VAST WISDOM

Inspiring You to Live Freely and Fully

Phara Lacombe

VAST WISDOM

Copyright © 2024 by Phara Lacombe

ISBN 979-8-218-25362-2

Published in the USA by MyPinga Publishing,
a subsidiary of FORTUNATELY FEMMES Inc.

Dedication

This book is dedicated, first and foremost, to my beloved sons, Leo and Alex. Thank you for your devoted belief in me and for encouraging me to rise above my self-doubts. Your wisdom, maturity, and kindness leave me in awe. I am endlessly proud of the men you are becoming, both with strong shoulders and generous hearts.

To my mother, my greatest inspiration and cheerleader—thank you for instilling in me the value of kindness and perseverance. Your belief that kindness always finds its way back has guided me through life's challenges.

A heartfelt dedication to Coach Betty Fortunat, an accomplished author and mentor, who saw a writer in me before I even realized it myself. You encouraged me to take this journey, and with patience and grace, you showed me how to bring my thoughts to the page at my own pace.

I also dedicate this work to myself, as it reflects my heart laid bare. Each page resonates with my joy, pain, highs, and lows, revealing my unique perspective on life.

And finally, to you, the reader. Your choice to explore these pages reflects your dedication to personal growth. My hope is that, by the end of this journey through 52 quotes, you will see the power in your thoughts and find deeper meaning in every decision, for your life matters greatly.

TABLE OF CONTENTS

INTRODUCTION

V ast Wisdom is not just a book; it's an invitation to rediscover your own potential, week by week. Within these pages, Phara Lacombe offers 52 transformative insights—each one crafted to unlock the strength and clarity within you. Each week, a new quote serves as a touchstone, gently guiding you toward freedom, resilience, and intentional living.

These are not merely inspirational words. Phara's reflections stir the heart and challenge the mind, urging you to question old limitations, embrace your power, and find beauty in self-discovery. With Vast Wisdom as your guide, each week becomes an opportunity to move forward with purpose, courage, and inner peace.

Let these words be a source of strength and a call to live expansively, joyfully, and authentically. As you journey through the year, may each quote awaken a new facet of your spirit and remind you of the vast, limitless potential that is uniquely yours.

LOVE YOUR LIFE, NO MATTER WHAT

"No matter how little you have, love your life. Embrace the opportunity of living your life each day."

As we begin this new year, let's ground ourselves in the greatest love—self-love—and in a spirit of deep gratitude. In a world that often measures worth by material wealth, it's easy to feel inadequate if we don't have everything we want. But true richness lies not in what we accumulate, but in our ability to appreciate what we already have. Life offers beauty in the simplest things: the warmth of a morning sun, the laughter of loved ones, or a moment of kindness. These are treasures available to us all, regardless of material possessions.

Starting the year with self-love means committing to see the value in each day, regardless of what we possess or lack. It's about embracing life's small, often overlooked joys and finding peace in simplicity. When we train ourselves to cherish what is already here, we unlock a new outlook—one that places less importance on what's missing and more on the blessings that surround us. This mindset builds resilience and fills us with grace, helping us to approach challenges with a heart full of strength and optimism.

Appreciating what you have doesn't deny life's hardships; instead, it helps you find meaning within them. Choosing to love yourself and value each moment fosters a gratitude that illuminates even life's darker corners. It reminds us that every day we wake up is a gift, each moment a chance to learn, connect, and grow.

This year, allow self-love and gratitude to guide your journey. Whether the road is rough or smooth, remember that the essence of life is not measured by abundance alone—it's a journey to be embraced and appreciated. Let gratitude be your foundation, love yourself well, and cherish what you have. In doing so, you will create a year filled with purpose, resilience, and peace.

Pause and Reflect

Week Two

THE POWER OF
PRAYER

"If you pray heavily at night,
you will feel lighter in the morning."

In the quiet hours of night, when the world rests and silence invite our hidden worries to surface, prayer becomes our refuge. We must surrender fully through prayer, to let go and let God. When we "pray heavily," it's not just a routine but a profound release—a shedding of burdens, a pouring out of everything weighing us down. It's a moment to bring our deepest fears, our unsolved questions, our fragile hopes, and lay them before Jehovah, asking for His divine protection, especially in times when we feel unsafe, uncertain, or confused. In these moments, the warmth of His presence is a powerful shield, a comfort in the storm.

Prayer is not just words spoken; it is a heartfelt transfer of our heaviest concerns, an acknowledgment that we are not meant to carry these alone. In prayer, we seek the protection only Jehovah can give, trusting that He sees beyond our fears and knows the paths that lie ahead. His love wraps around us like a strong embrace, a reminder that we are safe under His care. And there, in His presence, we discover a peace that softens even the sharpest worries, turning them into something we can bear.

This intentional act of "praying heavily" transforms us. It's not just our burdens that we release but also the illusion of control. In our surrender, we find a lightness of spirit, a liberation that allows us to awaken each morning with clarity and resilience. This lightness is the soul's way of healing, an invitation to begin the day unburdened and open, fully prepared to embrace whatever comes with strength and grace.

Prayer, then, becomes the doorway to renewal. It's the sacred practice that reshapes our perspective, filling our hearts with faith and freeing us from the demands of life's constant pressures. And as we bring our fears and uncertainties to Jehovah, we are not only seeking answers but receiving His unwavering assurance. Each time we "pray heavy," we step into the new day lighter, knowing that, with God by our side, we are protected and never truly alone. This act of surrender through prayer doesn't just change our nights; it renews us entirely, fortifying us for all that lies ahead.

Pause and Reflect

_____

_____

_____

_____

_____

_____

_____

_____

_____

_____

_____

_____

_____

_____

_____

_____

_____

_____

Chapter Three

RUN YOUR OWN RACE

"We often force the direction of our lives, failing to enjoy the paths along the way. The outside pressure of what is required at a certain age, often from people who've failed to meet the requirements they exacted from others, or perhaps appears to be meeting the requirements publicly but failing terribly in private. I encourage you to run your own race, so that you may arrive at your destination at your pace."

Life can feel like a race against the clock, with societal expectations dictating milestones. We rush to achieve predefined goals—whether it's graduating by a certain age, buying a house, or having a family—without appreciating the unique journeys that unfold. The pressure to conform often comes from people projecting their insecurities, including those who may not have achieved the very standards they impose on others. Some excel publicly while privately grappling with unfulfilled dreams, a reminder that appearances are deceptive.

In contrast, living authentically is about pacing yourself according to your values and priorities. Running your own race means setting realistic goals and milestones, not because others expect it but because it aligns with your purpose. It also means giving yourself permission to slow down, reflect, and enjoy life's beauty along the way. Progress looks different for everyone, and rushing ahead can rob us of meaningful experiences.

Your journey is not defined by others' timelines. Whether you take the scenic route or face detours, every step matters. In embracing your own path, you learn to honor your pace, arriving at your destination when it feels right. Ultimately, success isn't just about what you achieve but how you live. Living slowly, intentionally, and joyfully is its own form of success—one that leaves you fulfilled, regardless of where you finish.

Pause and Reflect

KEEP YOUR HEART FRESH

"

"Every now and then be sure to
examine your heart,
don't allow it to get stale."

The heart is the essence of who we are—our feelings, hopes, and intentions all stem from this core. But as time passes, life's disappointments, betrayals, and stresses can clutter our hearts, leaving us feeling burdened and disconnected. To truly live fully and openly, we need to start by releasing everything from previous years—let go of what's stale, tired, or weighed down. Keeping a fresh heart means choosing to cleanse, to remove the debris, and to breathe new life into our spirit. Just as you would prepare for a new day with fresh clothes, the heart needs to be renewed, stripped of its heaviness, and dressed in lightness and grace.

Refreshing your heart begins with the courage to let go. Release old grudges, practice forgiveness, and free yourself from lingering negativity that no longer serves you. This process is much like tending a garden; weeds of past hurts must be cleared so that new growth can flourish. A heart filled with past burdens grows stagnant, holding you back from experiencing the fullness of life. But when you actively nurture your heart, you keep it vibrant, open, and ready for fresh experiences.

To breathe new life into your heart, start by being honest with yourself. Are you holding on to beliefs, habits, or relationships that drain you? Are there patterns from the past year that no longer align with who you are becoming? Be intentional in making space for joy, gratitude, and genuine connections. Just as you would declutter a room to make space for something new, clearing your heart allows room for excitement and possibility.

Living with a fresh heart means approaching each day with curiosity, with a readiness for love and discovery. The process may ask you to be vulnerable, to confront pain or disappointment, but in doing so, you create a heart ready to bloom. And in that openness, you will find yourself more aligned with your deepest values, walking into each new season with clarity, purpose, and joy.

By regularly renewing our hearts, we step into life with a spirit that is light, refreshed, and always prepared to embrace the present. In each moment, we make room for new growth, inviting beauty, love, and fresh air into the core of who we are.

Pause and Reflect

Chapter Five

TEACHING COURAGE IN SIMPLICITY

"

"Teach your children how to live poor with courage versus rich with a lost soul."

The values we pour into our children's hearts shape not just the adults they'll become but the legacy they'll leave behind. In a society fixated on wealth and status, it is easy to believe that happiness has a price tag. Yet, material success without a foundation of integrity and purpose leaves a person feeling hollow, as if something vital is missing. True fulfillment lies not in riches but in a life lived with courage, honor, and meaning.

We need to bless our children with the gift of vast wisdom—a guiding compass—so they can make wise decisions, even when life's path becomes uncertain. This wisdom, rooted in courage and simplicity, goes beyond book knowledge. It's about teaching them to value relationships, creativity, and inner worth over the fleeting allure of material gains. Children who are grounded in these truths become resilient, emotionally strong, and self-aware, growing up to be responsible adults we can truly be proud of.

Living "poor with courage" embodies a mindset of gratitude, perseverance, and contentment. It teaches children that true wealth lies in character, not possessions. On the other hand, living "rich with a lost soul" serves as a warning: prioritizing external success at the cost of inner peace can lead to a life devoid of real joy. When our children carry these values in their hearts, they are equipped to weather life's ups and downs with integrity and resilience.

This lesson empowers them to pursue lives filled with purpose and meaning, whether material wealth follows. It teaches them that every decision, big or small, is an opportunity to choose what aligns with their core values, allowing them to build lives they are proud of.

Ultimately, this is the greatest gift we can give: a foundation of wisdom that lights their path, so they can face life's challenges with grace and confidence. Wealth may come, but the vast wisdom they carry within will be their true fortune, their legacy.

Pause and Reflect

THE TANGIBILITY OF "I LOVE YOU"

"*It is the actions that accompany 'I Love You' that makes it tangible.*"

As we enter February, the month known for love, let this be a time to show your love even more deeply. Words can be powerful, yes, but without action, they remain hollow. True love goes beyond declarations; it must be lived out through consistent, thoughtful gestures. Grand statements of affection hold little weight unless they are backed by kindness, patience, and genuine care. The real essence of love shows up in those small, everyday moments—helping without being asked, listening fully, showing up even when it's inconvenient.

Love is something we feel because it's something we see and experience. When someone says, "I love you," it becomes real through the way they prioritize your well-being, lend a hand in hard times, and choose honesty over convenience. Words might fade, but actions leave lasting impressions on the heart. It's in these moments, both big and small, that love transforms into something we can trust, something we believe in and depend on.

Tangible love requires intentionality. It's rarely convenient, and sometimes it's challenging, but it is always worth it. Love without action is like a seed left to wither—it cannot grow or thrive. But when actions align with words, love becomes more than just a feeling; it becomes the foundation of trust, connection, and healing.

So, this February, make a choice to live love out loud. Be intentional, be present, and let your actions speak just as loudly as your words. Show love in ways that build up the people around you and strengthen the bonds you hold dear. True love, after all, is a gift given daily through acts of kindness, a gift that speaks in volumes words alone could never capture.

Pause and Reflect

CHOOSING YOURSELF AND FALLING IN LOVE WITH YOUR LIFE

"

"I have put my heart in every aspect of my life, whether it was friendship, relationship, rearing children, work, tasks, and goals. I gave it my best. I gave it my time, my attention, overcompensated with support and affection, sometimes to people I barely knew; never any ill-agenda except to see people win and be happy. However, I can no longer be in any type of relationship where what I put in is not reciprocated as pure and free as what was received from me. I choose me now and I am falling in love with myself hard, because my life depends on it."

L iving with a giving heart often feels rewarding, but it can also become draining when the energy you invest in others isn't returned. Whether in relationships, friendships, or professional spaces, people with generous spirits often find themselves overextending—providing time, care, and emotional labor without receiving the same in return. This generosity may even extend to those we hardly know, with no hidden motives other than to see others succeed and feel joy. However, there comes a moment of clarity when one realizes that self-love must become the priority.

Choosing yourself is an act of reclamation. It means acknowledging that giving is beautiful, but it must have limits. Relationships thrive on reciprocity, where mutual support and affection sustain both parties. When you repeatedly pour yourself into spaces that do not nourish you in return, you risk losing sight of your own well-being. Falling in love with yourself is the antidote. It involves setting healthy boundaries and learning to prioritize your needs without guilt.

This decision is not selfish; it is essential. Your life depends on loving yourself deeply, affirming your worth, and being intentional about where you place your energy. When you choose yourself, you give yourself permission to grow, heal, and thrive. And as you cultivate this self-love, you attract relationships that honor and reflect the love you give.

Pause and Reflect

_____

_____

_____

_____

_____

_____

_____

_____

_____

_____

_____

_____

_____

_____

_____

_____

_____

Week Eight

OPTIONS AND CONNECTION

66

"In reality, we all have options until we meet someone special enough to rid all our options out. May you find your special person."

Love has a way of guiding us, simplifying our lives when we encounter that one person who makes all other options fade away. Life often presents a sea of choices, a vast array of potential paths and connections. Yet, love, in its purest form, arrives not to overwhelm but to clarify. When we find someone who resonates deeply with our spirit, suddenly, the noise quiets, and our heart chooses with a conviction that feels effortless. This is not mere attraction but a profound shift —a beautiful surrender from wandering to fully embracing.

Such a connection does not just happen; it emerges as we journey through self-discovery. By uncovering our own values and desires, we become equipped to recognize that rare, precious person when they appear. Each experience, every connection, shapes us, teaching us what we truly need. And when the right love arrives, it feels like coming home. Patience and openness guide us, for love worthy of commitment is built on the foundation of understanding both ourselves and our path.

There is courage in choosing love. Finding someone who makes us willing to set aside every other possibility requires vulnerability, trust, and faith. Love calls us to be brave, to let go of hesitation, and to embrace a future intertwined with another's. This leap of faith may feel daunting, but it is the doorway to joy, depth, and a life shared in the most profound way.

So, when that person enters your life, let yourself lean fully into that connection. May you cherish the journey of love—one that transforms your life by simplifying it, bringing clarity to your choices, and filling your soul with a love that was always worth waiting for. This is the ultimate wisdom of the heart: to recognize and cherish the rare gift of love that completes us.

Pause and Reflect

Week Nine

RELATIONSHIP WISDOM

❝

- *Breaking up is hard, but cheating is harder, not to mention disrespectful and it break trust. You can trust someone who breaks up with you, but you can't trust someone who cheats on you.*
- *Don't give in into temptation, once you do, it's hard to come back. Once you experience someone else you begin to take for granted what you once share with your partner.*
- *Sex is always great in the beginning, it is steamy, estatic and everything nice, but it will eventually fade, you need to revive sex with your partner, not replace your partner.*
- *Sex is not necessarily better without your partner, it's the rush of doing something that you know is wrong and getting away with it that creates the rush which makes it seem better.*
- *Sex doesn't get boring, partners not teaching each other something new, makes sex boring.*
- *Great sex are both people climaxing together and at the same time, I refer to it as the Power Ball, aim for that always.*
- *Love the person you're with, instead of imagining life or sex with some else. Imagination will sometimes lead you to pursue a reality, that you later wished was an imagination, but then it's too late.*
- *Ask yourself is it worth it, to throw away all that you have and have built with your partner, to experience sex with someone else."*

Navigating the complexities of relationships can be one of life's most challenging endeavors. The journey often involves heart-wrenching decisions, particularly when it comes to ending a relationship. Breaking up is undoubtedly difficult, but it is essential to recognize that cheating is an even greater betrayal. Trust, once broken, is challenging to rebuild, and it is crucial to differentiate between the two experiences. While ending a relationship may bring pain, it also opens the door to healing and growth. On the other hand, infidelity can shatter the very foundation of a relationship, leading to deep emotional scars that can linger long after the act itself.

The temptation to give in to momentary desires can often cloud our judgment. When we compromise our values for fleeting satisfaction, we not only risk our relationships but also undermine our self-worth. Relationships thrive on mutual respect, and succumbing to temptation can erode the trust that binds partners together. Recognizing this is vital; once trust is broken, it can be a long and arduous road back to intimacy. It is essential to build a solid foundation of honesty and loyalty, ensuring that both partners feel valued and secure. Establishing clear boundaries and maintaining open communication can help mitigate the risks of temptation and dishonesty.

As relationships evolve, so too does the nature of intimacy. In the early stages, passion often reigns supreme, characterized by excitement and novelty. However, as time progresses, it becomes necessary to nurture and reignite that initial flame. This doesn't mean seeking new partners but rather investing in your connection. Prioritizing intimacy, exploration, and vulnerability with your partner can revitalize your relationship, allowing both partners to grow together. It is crucial to remember that love requires effort and commitment. The rush of new experiences may fade, but the deep bond formed through shared moments and mutual understanding can create a lasting connection.

Lastly, it is vital to remain present in your relationship. Instead of fantasizing about an idealized version of love or intimacy, focus on cherishing the person before you. Discontent often arises from unrealistic expectations, leading us to overlook the beauty of our current relationships. It is essential to ask ourselves whether pursuing a fleeting thrill is worth sacrificing the meaningful connection we've cultivated.

The journey of love is not without its challenges, but by actively engaging with our partners, communicating our needs, and fostering a spirit of growth, we can navigate the complexities of love with grace and intention. Ultimately, embracing the imperfections and nurturing the bond we share can lead to a deeper, more fulfilling experience of love and connection.

Pause and Reflect

THE STRENGTH BENEATH THE SURFACE:
UNDERSTANDING THE TRUE ESSENCE OF RESILIENCE

"

"Oftentimes a man will tell a woman, 'You are strong,' as if to imply she is all set and doesn't need anything at all. Most strong women are overwhelmed, overworked, and overtired. They are strong not by choice but by the reality of having no one to catch them if they should fall. A strong woman should seek to be with a man who encourages her to put her strong hat down and fall back on him, both figuratively and literally. A man who allows her to be vulnerable, and a man who can assure her, 'I got you.' A man who says, 'You can be strong for the world, but for me,
I only want you to be yourself.'"

March, celebrated as Women's Month, calls us to honor not only the strength but the depth and complexity of the women around us. True strength does not exist without vulnerability; many women bear unseen burdens, navigating a world that often assumes they are unbreakable. Yet, resilience isn't about never needing support—it's about the courage to lean on others, even when expectations suggest they carry it all alone.

This month, we are reminded to embrace a new vision of partnership, one where women feel empowered to release the weight they carry. When men and women alike step into roles of compassion, they create spaces where armor can fall away, and authenticity can flourish. A strong partnership is not defined by independence alone, but by the mutual respect and empathy that allows each to lean on the other. In such a relationship, a woman can find comfort in knowing, "I've got you," does not lessen her strength—it amplifies it.

The greatest gift to a strong woman is a partner who encourages her to embrace her full, unfiltered self—dreams, fears, and all. When she finds solace in a partner who welcomes her whole truth, it creates a foundation of trust and deep connection. In this space, both partners are freed to grow and explore, without judgment or restraint, building a bond that celebrates both strength and softness.

This Women's Month, let us reframe our idea of resilience, honoring the quiet strength that comes with knowing we don't have to be unbreakable alone. True love and partnership thrive in the beauty of shared vulnerability, where both partners uplift each other's strengths and nurture each other's hearts. Together, they build a life that transcends expectation, rooted in a trust that is both fierce and tender, celebrating the fullness of being human and the profound grace of being loved.

Pause and Reflect

_____

_____

_____

_____

_____

_____

_____

_____

_____

_____

_____

_____

_____

_____

_____

_____

_____

_____

_____

_____

_____

_____

_____

Week Eleven

SEASONS OF GOODNESS AND ENDINGS

"It was good when it was good, it changed when it needed to end. Rely on God to set all matters straight in your life. God brings in what you need and removes what you do not need."

L ife unfolds in seasons, and every experience—good or challenging—has its time and purpose. When something is good, we savor it; we hold it close. But even the most beautiful things must come to an end when their time is up. This is not a tragedy but a necessary rhythm. The wisdom lies in knowing when to release what no longer serves us, trusting that God is at work behind the scenes. Holding on too tightly will only make transitions more painful but letting go with grace allows life to flow as it should.

God's hand in our lives means we don't always get to keep everything we want. He moves through our experiences, sometimes removing things that feel essential to us. Yet every subtraction in our life makes room for new blessings we may not even see coming. We must lean into faith, knowing that God only removes what we no longer need—even if, at the moment, it doesn't feel that way. It takes trust to believe that life is always setting us up for the next chapter of growth.

There is a divine precision in God's timing. When we stop resisting and allow things to unfold, we find peace. Sometimes endings appear harsh, but they are often God's way of clearing a path toward something better. Our job is not to question why things end but to be grateful for the time they served us. It is in the trusting and releasing that we align ourselves with God's will. When we surrender, we position ourselves to receive the new blessings meant for us.

Ultimately, life is a series of arrivals and departures, each with its meaning and purpose. It was good when it was good—and that's enough. Don't mourn the ending; instead, rejoice in the new beginning God is preparing. He is always in control, shifting things so you can grow, removing what burdens you, and bringing in what will elevate you. Trust in that process, for God is never late, and His plan is always perfect.

Pause and Reflect

_____

_____

_____

_____

_____

_____

_____

_____

_____

_____

_____

_____

_____

_____

_____

_____

_____

_____

_____

STANDING IN MY TRUTH AS A WOMAN

"

"I am super proud of the woman I am.

I love the woman I am.

I embrace the woman I am.

I genuinely admire the woman I am.

I am comfortable with the woman

I am.

I understand the woman I am."

As we celebrate Women's Month, let us stand tall in the power of self-confidence and honor the strength of knowing who we are. There is a quiet, unstoppable force in being rooted in our truth. Every woman's journey—her challenges, victories, and moments of growth—builds the foundation for the powerful soul she becomes. I have walked through storms and basked in blessings, each experience shaping me into the woman I am today. Self-pride is not arrogance; it is the recognition of resilience and growth, a silent gratitude for every battle fought and every lesson learned.

Loving myself has been the most transformative part of my journey. I have discovered that the love I once sought from others is most fulfilling when it comes from within. I look at myself not with a need for perfection but with genuine admiration. Every flaw, every triumph, every misstep—all are essential chapters in my story, and I embrace them all. I love the woman I am becoming because she is whole and real, defined by her own truth, not by anyone's expectations.

In a world that often pushes us to conform, there is freedom in self-acceptance. I have learned to walk confidently in my own skin because I know my worth. I no longer seek validation from others; I honor my strengths and extend grace to my weaknesses, knowing that every part of me is essential to my growth. This journey has no endpoint, only moments that bring me closer to the woman I am meant to be.

True peace lies in this unwavering self-love, this quiet contentment that comes from understanding and celebrating ourselves. When you reach this place, the opinions of others lose their grip, and you step forward, unshakable in the fullness of who you are. This Women's Month, let's embrace our journeys, trust our worth, and celebrate our stories. Because we are enough—exactly as we are, exactly where we are meant to be.

Pause and Reflect

FROM DEPTHS TO HEIGHTS:
EMBRACING DIVINE ELEVATION

"Glory to God, the one who dwells most high
but sees us at our very bottom and
elevates us to our highest form."

In His infinite power and boundless love, God is both beyond us and profoundly nearby. He is sovereign over all creation, yet intimately aware of each of our struggles and triumphs. This divine paradox speaks to a God who reigns from the highest place but is never too far to reach into our lowest moments. In seasons of failure, heartbreak, or uncertainty, God sees us fully. He does not turn away from our pain but instead steps into our lives with the grace and strength to elevate us beyond it.

This truth is a call to trust in the process of transformation, knowing that God's presence is not only a comfort but a catalyst. Though we may feel lost or overwhelmed, God's purpose weaves every trial into a step forward, a step upward. His hand lifts us, shaping our struggles into something new, something more resilient, leading us closer to the people He designed us to be. This is divine elevation—moving from where we are to where we're meant to be, carried by grace.

In times of struggle, it is easy to feel distant from our purpose, to believe we're beyond repair or too far gone for a new beginning. But God's love is not deterred by our circumstances. He does not wait for perfection; instead, He transforms us within our imperfections, drawing us from brokenness into wholeness, from weakness into strength. With God, even our valleys hold meaning, offering us fertile ground for growth and the promise of renewal.

This message encourages us to give thanks not only in moments of joy but also in times of hardship, for every experience contributes to the beautiful, complex tapestry of our lives. And in our gratitude, we recognize that God's grace is the constant that elevates us. We are reminded that God, who reigns above all, is also with us in our depths, transforming every moment, every challenge, into a part of our journey toward fullness and peace. Through this journey, we come to see that even in life's darkest valleys, there is light—His light—calling us to rise.

Pause and Reflect

TRUSTING GOD'S SIGHT AND TIMING

66

"God did not give us the ability to hear the good nor the bad in our absence; it's for His ears only. God didn't give us the ability to see the gifts intended for us nor the traps set for us; it is for His eyes only. However, He gave us the assurance that He would take care of matters with His own hand and resolve it in due time. In this assurance I dwell."

Life's mysteries are vast and humbling—the things left unsaid, the intentions unspoken, and the roads yet to unfold. It is natural to feel a pull toward control, to want a clear picture of what lies ahead, but here is where faith asks something more profound of us. True faith is not about knowing; it is about surrendering, about trusting that God, in His infinite wisdom, holds every piece of our lives in His capable hands. He did not design us to carry the full weight of understanding, nor did He grant us the power to control every circumstance. Some spaces are reserved for Him alone, hidden places where He works with boundless power and purpose on our behalf.

To trust God's plan is to acknowledge that some blessings and battles will remain unseen by us, yet wholly known to Him. It is trusting that His work is not limited by what we can comprehend. In the invisible, He crafts protection, solutions, and opportunities that would only weigh us down if we tried to carry them. His hand is there, guiding and shielding us from things beyond our sight—things we may never understand or even know to be grateful for. Faith is believing that every detail we lack, every mystery we don't understand, is being woven with love into the fabric of our lives.

Living with this assurance is liberating. It frees us from the need to micromanage, question, and doubt every step. Faith lets us release the weight of our worries and the need to control outcomes, resting instead in the truth that God's vision is clearer, His timing is flawless, and His plan is for our good. In surrendering the unknown, we find a deeper peace—a peace that transcends every unanswered question and quells every anxious thought. In this surrender, we allow God to be God, and we allow ourselves to simply *be*; to walk forward with courage, to embrace each day with trust, and to rest in the knowledge that our journey is already in the hands of a faithful Creator.

Faith in God's unseen work invites us into a life of calm assurance. Even when the path is obscured and life feels uncertain, we can rest, knowing that His hand is steady. In His own time, what we need will come to us; what we don't will fall away. We can trust that He is aligning each step, each season, to fulfill His promises. As we let go of the need to see and control it all, our souls find the profound rest that only a surrendered life can bring. In this trust, we find not just peace but freedom—the freedom to live each moment with open hands and a heart that knows: with God, all is, indeed, well.

Pause and Reflect

RESPECT FOR DIFFERENT LIFE CHOICES

> "Respect the rights of those who choose to live life more conservatively, so those whom you say are too conservative can also respect your rights to live life more loosely."

The beauty of life lies in its diversity. We all approach it from different angles—some guided by structure and restraint, others by freedom and spontaneity. Neither path is inherently right or wrong, only reflective of individual journeys. Respecting others' choices, especially when they differ from ours, is an essential part of living harmoniously. Just as we desire the freedom to live on our own terms, we must extend that freedom to others.

True respect is not about agreement; it's about coexistence. It's recognizing that everyone walks their unique path based on values, experiences, and personal convictions. A conservative life may seem limiting to some, just as a loose, unstructured life may appear reckless to others. But the common thread between both is the right to choose. Respect allows people to feel seen and honored, even when their paths diverge.

Judging someone else's lifestyle can create unnecessary divisions, but mutual respect builds bridges. When we choose to honor someone's choices—even if they do not align with ours—we foster an environment where differences are celebrated, not condemned. In this exchange, understanding grows, and respect becomes the foundation for unity.

Pause and Reflect

MIND YOUR TIME

"Stay out of conversations unless you can bring value to it, or it brings value to you. If you can't upbuild, empathize, learn from, teach, correct, or advise; don't allow that conversation to drain your time.

Mind your time."

Time is a finite resource, and how we use it determines the trajectory of our lives. Every conversation carries an opportunity to build or break—whether it strengthens connections or diminishes energy. If the words exchanged leave no room for growth, understanding, or encouragement, they become distractions. Life becomes more purposeful when we engage intentionally, pouring value into the dialogue or receiving it. When conversations turn into idle noise, they not only steal moments but also deplete focus.

True wisdom comes from knowing which discussions to embrace and which to release. It is not avoidance; it is discernment. Conversations are vessels for empathy and learning, but not every exchange deserves your presence. To 'mind your time' is not about selfishness but stewardship—treating time as the precious gift it is. Guard your hours like treasures, because each wasted conversation is an opportunity lost.

In this light, consider every word you share or absorb. Are you adding light to someone's path, gaining insight, or nurturing relationships? If not, let the silence be your friend. Choose intentionality over obligation—give your energy only where it aligns with your purpose. When you become selective with your time, you unlock more of it to devote to things that truly matter.

Pause and Reflect

Week Seventeen

Week Seventeen

LIVING HONESTLY AND AUTHENTICALLY

66

"Live your truth. SOME are not living their truth, why do you commit to a monogamous relationship when your heart is drawn towards polygamy, subjecting a monogamous partner to lies and deceits?"

Living honestly is not just about telling the truth; it is about living in alignment with who you are. Too often, people force themselves into roles or relationships that don't reflect their truth because they fear judgment or rejection. But wearing a mask—whether in love or life—only leads to pain. If your heart craves freedom, why bind yourself to a life that requires constant lies to maintain the illusion of commitment? A monogamous partner deserves truth, not deceit, and you deserve the freedom to live authentically.

There is no shame in knowing your desires, even if they do not fit societal norms. The real harm comes when you deny your truth and drag others into the deception. When you enter a monogamous relationship with a heart drawn toward polygamy, you set the stage for betrayal. Not only do you hurt your partner, but you also imprison yourself in a life that feels like a lie. Honesty is hard, but it's the only way to build relationships on trust and respect.

Living your truth means making choices that align with who you are and giving others the same freedom. It requires courage to step away from the expectations others place on you, but the reward is a life of peace. It is better to face uncomfortable truths early than to live a life of pretense. Integrity in relationships is not just about fidelity—it's about transparency and giving your partner the respect they deserve by being truthful from the start.

In the end, living authentically is an act of liberation. When you walk in truth, you free yourself from the burden of lies and give others the opportunity to choose their path honestly. A relationship built on anything less than truth will always crumble under the weight of deception. But when you honor your truth, you create space for genuine love—whatever form that may take.

Pause and Reflect

CHOOSING LOVE OVER BITTERNESS

"During a very difficult time in my life, I asked God for love. You may wonder why love, why not ask for endurance. Throughout my life, I have seen so many people endure. Endurance got them through, but they were left bitter. I wanted a healed heart, the freedom of living life without resentment. The ability to forgive and look past the fault of others, to separate their good attributes from their bad decisions. Love has taught me to endure, I am not confident endurance could have taught me to love."

When life pressed me to the edge, I did not ask for the strength to simply survive—I asked God for love. Love, after all, does more than carry you through; it transforms you. Love teaches you how to forgive, how to see the light in people even when they've hurt you, and how to release resentment from your heart.

Endurance gets you through the storm, but it does not always leave you whole. I've known people who endured life's hardest trials only to emerge bitter, weighed down by what they had to suffer. I knew that path wasn't for me. I wanted to heal, to live free of the anger that life's challenges can create. Love gave me that freedom. It allowed me to look beyond the mistakes of others and see the goodness that still lived within them.

Love taught me to endure, but it also did more—it taught me to heal. It showed me that life's difficulties do not have to define us. With love, I found the strength to forgive not just others but myself. I learned to let go of the need for revenge or justice and instead embrace the peace that comes with acceptance. Endurance may keep you standing, but love gives you the grace to move forward without bitterness.

In the end, love is what made me whole. It taught me that true endurance is not just about surviving hardship, but about living with an open heart after the storm has passed. I do not regret asking God for love. It gave me everything I needed: peace, forgiveness, and the ability to live free. And in that freedom, I found my greatest strength.

Pause and Reflect

Week Nineteen

FLYING IN A FALLING WORLD

"

May you fly

May you fly in the decisions you make

May you fly in the goals you've set forth

May you fly in your resolve to never give up,

to love profoundly, and trust wholeheartedly

May you fly with a happy smile.

May you always fly, in this falling world.

As we enter May, a month of renewal and growth, may you soar above life's challenges with unwavering intention and grace. May this be the season you rise, shedding the weight of hesitation and fear, aligning yourself boldly with the dreams that stir your soul. To "fly" is not merely to reach new heights but to navigate life's complexities with courage, to embrace each lesson, and to persist despite the unknowns. It is about reaching upward, evolving continuously, and staying true to who you are as you push forward toward both personal fulfillment and purposeful ambition.

This journey asks for inner resolve—a commitment to move forward even when the path is unclear, or obstacles arise. True strength lies in that choice: the decision to keep going, fueled by a heart full of love and trust. To soar isn't just about what we achieve; it's about nurturing our spirit and relationships, even when life feels unsteady. Embracing love wholeheartedly, despite past disappointments, and trusting in the goodness that life still offers, are acts of profound bravery. Each step forward is a testament to our resilience, a reminder that soaring requires both faith and persistence.

The call to "fly with a happy smile" reminds us that joy is not an afterthought but an essential companion on this journey. Success means little without a sense of lightness. To carry joy —even through trials—is to show gratitude for the journey itself, rather than only its destination. Smiling in the face of life's ups and downs keeps us grounded in what truly matters, in the beauty and meaning embedded in each moment. This joy sustains us, providing balance as we continue to rise.

And yes, we soar within an imperfect world, one often marked by struggle and loss. But to fly is to embrace that imperfection and rise above it. The world may be in flux, full of uncertainties, yet we can still choose to elevate ourselves, to find strength in our purpose and joy in our journey. May you fly high this month, lifted by hope, love, trust, and an unyielding belief in the beauty that awaits. You were meant to soar, even as the world falls—because the power within you knows no bounds.

Pause and Reflect

Week Twenty

THE GRACE OF PERSPECTIVE:
EMBRACING LIFE'S CHALLENGES WITH TRUST AND COMPASSION

"

"It could always be worse when it's not what you want. It could always be worse when it doesn't go as planned. It isn't the worst case ever; somewhere in the universe, someone is dealing with something far worse. I am constantly saying these sentences as a reminder to myself that while certain outcomes may be different than what is desired, there's so much ahead to look forward to. Learning to cope with what you do not desire is living a balanced life. It is also about trusting God's timing and understanding that far beyond your desires, God knows what's best for you, and he will work things in your favor though it may look bleak at times, but you must first believe in the goodness of God as you continue to strive towards your desires."

Often, disappointment feels inevitable. We build dreams, chart plans, and envision outcomes, only to watch life twist and turn beyond our control. But there is profound wisdom in understanding that the universe, in its vastness, operates on a rhythm that surpasses our own. This reflection speaks to the heart of resilience: that even in our moments of dissatisfaction, there lies a truth we must not ignore—things could indeed be worse. Recognizing this truth is an invitation to foster gratitude, a call to shift our gaze from what is absent to the abundance surrounding us.

As we walk through life's unpredictable pathways, we must remember we are not alone in our struggles. Somewhere, someone is facing burdens even heavier than ours. This universal truth connects us, cultivating compassion and humility as we navigate our own difficulties. Embracing this perspective is not about dismissing our pain but finding balance—acknowledging our disappointments while also embracing the quiet promise that better days are coming.

Learning to live with what we do not desire is not passive; it is a powerful stance, an active choice to engage with life as it unfolds. This journey requires us to trust in divine timing, to believe in a wisdom greater than our own. God, in His boundless understanding, knows our hearts better than we do and, in His grace, gives us what we need rather than what we may demand. This reflection reminds us to lean into that trust, surrendering to the mystery of what lies ahead, convinced of the goodness waiting beyond our current view.

When the road feels long and hope seems distant, let us anchor ourselves in the resilience we already possess. With a heart open to growth and renewal, we shift our mindset, welcoming the possibilities that await. The journey may challenge us, but with faith as our guide, we are not only prepared to weather the storms; we are poised to emerge stronger, wiser, and ever more attuned to the blessings we are destined to encounter.

Pause and Reflect

_____

_____

_____

_____

_____

_____

_____

_____

_____

_____

_____

_____

_____

_____

_____

_____

_____

_____

_____

_____

THE RIPPLE EFFECT OF LOVE:
NURTURING POSITIVE CONNECTIONS THROUGH OUR WORDS

"Love often starts from seeing how others love a person. Consider this: a child will grow to admire and love your favorite ball player, singer, movie star, or a friend, because they listen to your expressions about that person, and they begin to love them like how you love them. They begin to admire their talents the way you admire it. In time, they become big fans of that person, their little face lights up over the slightest possibility of meeting a stranger who's celebrated at home for playing a great game or who sings well on TV. We can help others create positive and loving perceptions about others, all depending on our speech. I hope you are using your power of speech to sow love, unity, and respect for others."

Love is a seed sown through the expressions we share, often germinating in the hearts of those who observe us. This reflection eloquently illustrates how our words shape the perceptions others hold of people in our lives. The profound impact of our speech becomes especially evident when we witness a child's innocent admiration for someone we cherish. Their ability to reflect our sentiments speaks to the heart of human connection, where love becomes a tapestry woven from shared experiences and expressions.

As we navigate our relationships, we wield a powerful tool—the ability to influence how others perceive the world around them. The words we choose to express our feelings can either foster admiration or breed misunderstanding. By consciously choosing to speak positively about others, we create an environment rich in love, unity, and respect. This practice not only elevates those we admire but also enhances our own capacity for love, deepening the connections we share with one another.

This reflection encourages us to be mindful of our speech, recognizing that it holds the power to create ripples of positivity. In a world that often grapples with division and discord, the act of showing love through our words can serve as a beacon of hope. By nurturing a culture of appreciation and respect, we empower others to recognize the beauty in those around them. Let us harness the power of our expressions to uplift, encourage, and inspire, ensuring that love flows freely from our lips to the hearts of others.

Pause and Reflect

NAVIGATING DISAGREEMENT WITH GRACE:
THE POWER OF LEAVING ROOM FOR LOVE

"

"Disagree without hate. Conclude without hate. Move on without hate. Always leave room for love to make its way in; in time, it may very well do."

In a world often characterized by discord and division, the ability to disagree without hate is a testament to emotional maturity and wisdom. This reflection encapsulates a powerful truth: conflict is a natural part of human interaction, yet it does not have to erode the foundations of love and respect. The call to engage in disagreement gracefully serves as a reminder that our responses shape the outcomes of our interactions.

When we disagree, it is essential to approach the situation with an open heart and mind. This means acknowledging differing perspectives while consciously choosing to avoid vitriol and animosity. By cultivating a mindset that values understanding over hostility, we create space for constructive dialogue, allowing for the possibility of reconciliation and growth. Concluding discussions without hate reinforces the idea that our relationships matter more than our need to be right.

The journey does not end with disagreement; it extends to moving on without carrying the burdens of anger or resentment. This reflection invites us to release the weight of negativity, leaving room for love to seep back into our interactions. When we embrace this principle, we cultivate an environment where healing can flourish, and connections can deepen.

Ultimately, this wisdom encourages us to engage with empathy and compassion, reminding us that the potential for love resides even in the most challenging conversations. As we practice this art of disagreement, we become architects of a more harmonious world, where understanding triumphs over division, and love reigns supreme.

Pause and Reflect

THE GIFT OF GENEROSITY: A HEARTFELT CONNECTION BEYOND COMPARISON

"Whether someone has more than you or less than you, do not dwell on that; give them a gift when your heart tells you to, because that person may have everything except a gift from you."

The act of giving transcends material wealth and social status. This reflection beautifully captures the essence of generosity: it is not about what we possess, but rather the love and kindness we choose to share. When we release ourselves from the chains of comparison—be it more or less—we open our hearts to the profound joy that comes from giving.

Too often, we find ourselves assessing our worth based on what we have compared to others. However, this mindset detracts from the beauty of connection that can blossom through the simple act of gifting. The invitation here is to listen to our hearts and respond to the whispers of generosity, recognizing that our contributions can make a significant impact, no matter how small they may seem.

The reminder that someone may have everything except a gift from us serves as a poignant call to action. The gifts we offer—be they tangible or intangible—carry the power to uplift spirits and forge deeper bonds. When we give from a place of love, we create ripples of positivity that extend far beyond ourselves.

You are invited to cultivate a spirit of generosity, allowing our hearts to guide our actions. As we embrace the beauty of giving without conditions, we enrich not only the lives of those we touch but also our own. Ultimately, the true essence of wealth lies not in what we accumulate but in the love we share and the connections we nurture along the way.

Pause and Reflect

HEALING AFTER A DIVORCE

"

"How to heal a broken heart that leads to divorce?

- Time
- Self-love
- Reflection
- Cry
- Grieve
- Embrace your vulnerability
- Forgive with or without an apology
- Learn a new hobby or pick up an old hobby to pass time
- Develop your talents
- Pursue dreams that you had placed on hold
- Acknowledge your worth
- Believe in the greatness the future holds
- Remember: 'God is close to the brokenhearted.' - Ps. 34:18 'He binds their wounds.' - Ps. 147:3"

Healing from divorce is a journey—one that requires patience, compassion, and intentionality. It is not just about the end of a relationship but also about rediscovering yourself and redefining your future. Time becomes your ally as it softens the sharp edges of pain and allows room for reflection. Self-love is essential during this period; it is about nurturing yourself and reclaiming your worth.

Grieving is part of the healing process. Tears, sadness, and moments of vulnerability are not signs of weakness but acts of release. It's in these moments that forgiveness also takes root —sometimes with an apology, and sometimes without one. Forgiveness is less about the other person and more about freeing yourself from bitterness.

As time passes, new opportunities emerge. Old hobbies reignite joy, and hidden talents surface. Dreams once set aside begin to feel attainable again. Most importantly, faith becomes the anchor through it all. Trusting that God is near, especially in moments of heartache, provides the strength to keep moving forward. Healing is not linear, but with every step, a brighter future awaits.

Pause and Reflect

_____

_____

_____

_____

_____

_____

_____

_____

_____

_____

_____

_____

_____

_____

_____

_____

_____

_____

THE CYCLE OF CHASING

❝

"You're chasing a new girl while your wife is at home; a new man is chasing your wife while you're out chasing a new girl. Finally, may the best chaser win."

Chasing a new partner can seem like an exciting adventure, filled with the promise of novelty and the allure of fresh beginnings. Yet, this pursuit often comes with hidden costs that we may not fully recognize now.

Love is sometimes treated as a game, it's all too easy to lose ourselves in the rush of the chase, mistaking excitement for connection. When we are chasing something newer or shinier, we are often overlooking the people who genuinely care for us, who offer stability and authenticity. Ironically, as we pursue these distractions, we may unknowingly push our partners into a similar search for fulfillment elsewhere. What results is a society filled with people constantly chasing, yet rarely finding real satisfaction—a world of hearts longing for true connection but endlessly caught in a loop of seeking.

This insight calls us to pause and examine our motives. Are we chasing because we desire adventure, or are we earnestly seeking connection? Often, we risk losing meaningful relationships for the sake of temporary attention. There is deep wisdom in understanding that genuine fulfillment often comes from nurturing the bonds we already have, from focusing on the depth of relationships rather than seeking the thrill of validation in fleeting encounters.

As we navigate our personal relationships, awareness is essential. Ask yourself: What do you truly value? The thrill of novelty, or the depth of a connection? True satisfaction in relationships isn't found in capturing fleeting attention but in investing love, time, and energy into someone who has been there all along. In the end, it is not about who wins the chase; it is about building enduring connections that stand the test of time.

Take, for example, the story of Balthazar, whose recent scandal revealed his pursuit of over 400 women while in a committed marriage. This relentless chase for new connections not only betrayed his relationship but also left him at the mercy of fleeting attention that was never truly satisfied. His actions underscore a larger truth: while the thrill of pursuit might promise excitement, it often ends in emptiness, leaving behind a trail of broken connections and trust.

Chase true connection, not distraction - a vast wisdom principle.

Pause and Reflect

_____
_____
_____
_____
_____
_____
_____
_____
_____
_____
_____
_____
_____
_____
_____
_____
_____
_____

THE EMPTY
DECISIONS

"There are decisions you make for the sake of keeping your sanity, but it leaves you feeling empty at times."

Life often presents us with choices that test the balance between mental clarity and emotional satisfaction. This insight captures the fine line we tread when deciding what to prioritize. Sometimes, we are drawn to choices that preserve our peace and shield us from turmoil, giving us the space to breathe and find calm. However, these choices can sometimes feel hollow, leaving us with an unfulfilled ache where our deeper desires reside. This is the challenge: we must honor our need for sanity without ignoring our heart's true longings.

In difficult times, self-preservation may lead us to choose safety over growth, sidestepping the discomfort that accompanies profound change. Yet, this avoidance can prevent us from experiencing the rich, fulfilling aspects of life that lie on the other side of discomfort. The wisdom here reminds us to reflect on our motives—are we safeguarding our peace, or are we evading the risks that lead to growth? True fulfillment often lies in choices that invite us to confront our fears and, in doing so, expand our potential.

To reconcile these feelings of emptiness is to acknowledge them openly, a necessary step in healing. We need to reconnect with what matters most, daring to prioritize choices that both uplift our spirit and protect our peace. Seeking harmony between our mental stability and emotional fulfillment is not about settling but about leaning into vulnerability, knowing that only then can we fill the void that self-preservation alone cannot fill.

May we always choose paths that feed our spirit and elevate our soul, for in the pursuit of true passion and alignment lies life's deepest satisfaction—a guiding principle of *Vast Wisdom*.

Pause and Reflect

THE HIDDEN MOTIVES

"

"Perhaps when they're going out of their way to convince you not to like someone, is when you should make an effort to find out for yourself."

I urge you to recognize that strength and wisdom lie in our ability to think independently and to connect authentically. Every day, we encounter opinions shaped by others' fears, past hurts, and sometimes, limited perspectives. They may mean well; they may think they are protecting us. But ultimately, these outside influences can cloud our judgment and block us from discovering something meaningful. In listening to others' doubts, we risk missing out on experiences that could bring joy, growth, or a deeper understanding of ourselves and the world around us.

When we choose to take life into our own hands, we choose to trust our instincts, to see the world not through someone else's lens but through our own. This is not just about relationships; it's about claiming ownership over our entire life path. Imagine the resilience that comes from making choices that reflect our truth, rather than trying to fit into another's expectations. Real fulfillment comes not from following the voices around us but from honoring the voice within us.

Each time we make a conscious choice to engage openly, to learn for ourselves, we strengthen our courage and build our empathy. By choosing to connect on our own terms, we learn the invaluable lesson that human beings are complex, that there's often more to people than others may see. True relationships form when we look past labels, and this kind of understanding brings not only deeper connection but also profound inner peace.

So, be bold. Seek truth in the face of societal norms, peer pressure, and doubt. Stand firm in your quest for clarity and wisdom, even when others project their uncertainty onto you. Each connection, each experience is a part of your journey, chosen by you. This courage to live by your own convictions will build a life rooted in honesty and depth. Embrace this wisdom, knowing that every step you take in this direction will lead to authenticity.

Let this principle become your guiding light, a reminder of the *Vast Wisdom* that comes from living fully, independently, and with open-hearted purpose.

Pause and Reflect

Week Twenty Eight

THE WEIGHT OF NEGATIVITY

"

"Sitting here, thinking DANG, life is heavy, yet some enjoy all the negative energy that makes it heavy. Give me love, positivity, encouragement, inspiration & motivation; anything less, you can keep."

Life can indeed feel overwhelming, filled with challenges and obstacles that threaten to drain our spirit. Yet, amidst this heaviness, it is crucial to recognize our power to choose the energy we invite into our lives. While some individuals may thrive in chaos and negativity, we must consciously seek out love, positivity, and inspiration as our guiding forces.

The weight of life can be daunting, but how we respond to that weight defines our experiences. Choosing to embrace positivity does not imply ignoring hardships; rather, it is about acknowledging our struggles and seeking the light that exists even in darkness. This quote serves as a powerful reminder of the importance of surrounding ourselves with uplifting influences that nurture our well-being and inspire us to rise above challenges.

As we navigate life's complexities, we must actively cultivate a mindset that prioritizes encouragement and motivation. Seek out relationships and environments that foster growth, love, and positivity. When we open ourselves to these energies, we become beacons of light, capable of sharing that warmth with others. The world can often feel heavy, but we have the power to shift our focus and inspire change—both within ourselves and in the lives of those around us.

In essence, choose wisely what you allow to occupy your mental space. Surround yourself with love, encouragement, and inspiration. The world can be a heavy place, but you have the agency to lighten the load through your choices and mindset.

Pause and Reflect

THE STRENGTH OF CHILDREN

"

"Drawing strength from your children is an unbelievable experience, it's an experience that is sure to change your whole life trajectory. You gain purpose and why becomes crystal clear. "

Drawing strength from your children is an unbelievable experience; it has the power to change your whole life trajectory. Children have a unique ability to inspire and motivate us in ways we may never have imagined. Their innocence, curiosity, and unwavering love remind us of what truly matters. Amid life's chaos, when we feel lost or overwhelmed, our children often become our guiding light, illuminating the path toward purpose. They possess an innate wisdom that encourages us to be better, to strive harder, and to pursue our dreams with relentless passion.

As we nurture and care for them, we begin to realize that our lives are no longer just our own. We gain purpose, and our "why" becomes crystal clear. Every sacrifice we make, every decision we ponder, is no longer solely for ourselves but for the future we wish to create for them. This transformative journey teaches us the importance of resilience, patience, and unconditional love. Each milestone they reach becomes a reflection of our commitment to them, reminding us of the legacy we wish to leave behind.

This profound connection challenges us to rethink our values and priorities. In moments of hardship or self-doubt, it is often the thought of our children that reignites our determination. Their laughter, their dreams, and their potential push us to overcome obstacles we once deemed insurmountable. It is a reminder that we are not just shaping their lives but that they, in turn, are shaping ours. The experience of drawing strength from our children is a beautiful cycle, where love and growth are shared, creating a foundation that fortifies our existence.

The love we invest in our children ultimately enriches our lives, creating a bond that transcends time and space. As we witness their growth and evolution, we find ourselves transformed in the process. Their presence serves as a powerful reminder that, through them, we can rediscover the beauty of life, purpose, and love.

Pause and Reflect

THE POWER OF GOODNESS

"*Be good, because you believe in the power of Good.*

Be good, because it's impactful and it's bigger than yourself.

Be good, because it's healing to yourself and others.

Be good, because you believe the world needs goodness, and it should start with you."

B e good, because you believe in the power of Good. Goodness is not just an act; it's a philosophy, a way of being that transcends our daily interactions. When we choose to embody goodness, we create ripples that extend far beyond ourselves. It's a reminder that our actions can inspire others, promoting a cycle of positivity that uplifts the entire community. When we act out of kindness and compassion, we align ourselves with a higher purpose, contributing to the collective good of humanity.

Be good, because it's impactful and it's bigger than yourself. The impact of goodness is profound, often felt in ways we may not immediately recognize. Each time we extend a helping hand or offer a word of encouragement, we contribute to a culture of empathy and understanding. In a world that can often feel divided, choosing to be good becomes a radical act of resistance against negativity and despair. It reaffirms our belief that love and kindness can prevail, reminding us that we each have the power to make a difference.

Be good, because it's healing to yourself and others. In the act of giving and being kind, we often find our own wounds begin to heal. Compassionate actions allow us to connect with others on a deeper level, fostering relationships rooted in understanding and support. This exchange of goodness not only lifts those around us but also nourishes our own spirit. It reinforces the idea that, in giving, we receive—creating a cycle of love that transcends boundaries and brings us closer together.

Be good, because you believe the world needs goodness, and it should start with you. Each of us carries the responsibility to foster a culture of goodness in our own lives. It begins with recognizing the power of our choices and the impact they have on our surroundings. By consciously choosing to be a force for good, we cultivate an environment where compassion flourishes and love prevails. The journey may be challenging at times, but the rewards are immeasurable. Let us commit to being the change we wish to see, starting with the goodness that resides within us.

Pause and Reflect

THE COST OF INTEGRITY

"

"It is not a surprise as why the honest remain poor and the greedy grow rich. Having integrity often means taking the long way, it often means going without before you can gain. It can equal suffering and what appears to be humiliation. However, integrity is the richest quality you can possess. It means you are selfless; you can be trusted; it also means you can withstand affliction. I pray the mighty God bless those with integrity today."

It is not a surprise as why the honest remain poor and the greedy grow rich. In a world often driven by materialism and self-interest, integrity can feel like a costly endeavor. Choosing the path of honesty and virtue frequently requires us to make sacrifices, to forgo immediate gratification for the sake of our principles. The journey of integrity is not always easy; it can be fraught with challenges and moments of doubt. Yet, it is during these trials that our character is truly tested, and our commitment to doing what is right becomes a beacon of hope in a world that can sometimes feel dark.

Having integrity often means taking the long way; it often means going without before you can gain. There will be times when the choices we make for the sake of integrity lead us to face adversity, and we may find ourselves at odds with the world around us. Yet, these moments are opportunities for growth and self-discovery. They teach us resilience, instilling a sense of strength that cannot be easily shaken. While the road may be long and lonely at times, we must remember that our integrity is a treasure far greater than material wealth.

However, integrity is the richest quality you can possess. It means you are selfless; you can be trusted, and it also means you can withstand affliction. In a world that often prioritizes shortcuts and quick wins, being a person of integrity is a radical choice. It speaks to our character and our commitment to truth, justice, and compassion. Those who walk this path may face hardships, but they also experience profound fulfillment, knowing they are living authentically. I pray the mighty God bless those with integrity today, for they are the true heroes of our society, paving the way for a brighter future.

Integrity transforms us from within, shaping not just our actions but our hearts. It reminds us that while the world may reward the dishonest, the true measure of wealth lies in our ability to remain true to ourselves and to others. Let us embrace integrity as our guiding principle, even when it's difficult, for in doing so, we not only uplift ourselves but also inspire those around us to seek the truth and live with purpose.

Pause and Reflect

CONTROL WHAT YOU CAN

"

"Life is truly what you make it to some extent. So, the part that is within your control, control it. Take control over anger, abusive speech, fights, gossip. Control your energy especially when you feel it unraveling in a negative way. Take breaks, sleep on it, put it off, almost every situation can be dealt with later. Control all things that require your decisions and reactions, don't let those things control you."

Life is truly what you make it to some extent. So, the part that is within your control, control it. It is essential to recognize that while we cannot dictate every aspect of our lives, we do hold the power to influence certain elements. Understanding where our control lies enables us to take charge of our reactions, decisions, and ultimately, our happiness. Each moment presents an opportunity to choose our responses, shaping the narrative of our lives in ways that align with our values and aspirations.

Take control over anger, abusive speech, fights, and gossip. These negative energies can drain us, leaving us feeling depleted and unfulfilled. By exercising self-control, we empower ourselves to break free from the cycles of negativity that threaten to engulf us. When we learn to pause, reflect, and choose our words and actions wisely, we create a space for growth and understanding. This mindfulness fosters healthier relationships and a more peaceful existence, allowing us to navigate life's challenges with grace and poise.

Control your energy, especially when you feel it unraveling in a negative way. Recognizing when we are spiraling into negativity is crucial; it allows us to take proactive steps to ground ourselves. Whether through meditation, seeking support from loved ones, or engaging in activities that bring us joy, we can redirect our energy toward more positive outlets. This practice not only promotes our well-being but also sets a precedent for those around us, encouraging a culture of positivity and resilience.

Almost every situation can be dealt with later. Control all things that require your decisions and reactions; don't let those things control you. Life is a series of choices, and it is our responsibility to approach each decision with intention. By taking the time to reflect before responding, we empower ourselves to make choices that align with our true selves. In this way, we reclaim our agency, crafting a life that reflects our values, desires, and aspirations. Let us be the masters of our reactions, cultivating a life that is not only meaningful but also fulfilling.

Pause and Reflect

Week Thirty Three

BREAKING GENERATIONAL CHAINS

"Breaking generational curse/chain is not easy, but it can be done. It starts with how we raised our children, especially those of us raising young men. Ensure you are having this conversation with your sons, I do. I hold a responsibility for how my son will treat your daughter, I can shape his mind now, so he understands your daughter is his sister by humanity and so when he takes her on another level, he must see her worth. If he cannot see her worth, leave her for someone else. Men are gentle and kind. You come from a woman."

Breaking generational curses and chains is not easy, but it can be done. It starts with how we raise our children, especially those of us raising young men. This task carries immense weight and responsibility. The conversations we have with our children today will shape the men and women they become tomorrow. We must be intentional about instilling values that promote kindness, respect, and understanding, particularly in our sons. Our dialogue can break the cycles of disrespect and entitlement that have plagued generations past.

Ensure you are having this conversation with your sons; I do. I hold a responsibility for how my son will treat your daughter. This awareness compels us to examine our beliefs and actions. We must model the behavior we wish to see in them, teaching them that every individual deserves respect and dignity. It is essential that they understand their role in fostering healthy relationships based on mutual respect and admiration. This is not merely about instilling fear or obedience; it is about nurturing a sense of responsibility and empathy.

I can shape his mind now, so he understands your daughter is his sister by people. This understanding is crucial, as it encourages our sons to recognize the intrinsic value of every person. When we help them see the world through this lens, we prepare them to engage in relationships that honor humanity in one another. Teaching our children to appreciate the worth of others fosters a culture of kindness that transcends individual interactions and builds a more compassionate society.

When he takes her on another level, he must see her worth. If he cannot see her worth, leave her for someone else. This simple yet profound principle encapsulates the essence of what it means to respect and honor another person. As parents, we have the power to shape not just the attitudes of our children but the future of relationships for generations to come. We must instill in them the understanding that love is built on mutual respect, admiration, and the recognition of each person's inherent value. Men can be gentle and kind; they are products of their environment and upbringing. When we raise them with this understanding, we break the chains of past injustices and pave the way for healthier, more respectful relationships.

In teaching our sons this vital lesson, we not only empower them but also contribute to the creation of a world where love, kindness, and respect are paramount. This is our legacy—the seeds we plant today will bloom into a more compassionate tomorrow. Let us strive to break the generational chains, forging a path where respect and love reign supreme, ensuring that the next generation embodies the values that promote unity and understanding.

Pause and Reflect

Week Thirty Four

FINDING MYSELF
IN THE PIECES

"

"Like a puzzle, I keep finding myself, missing pieces scattered but not lost. No longer anxious to fill in the missing pieces, more eager to learn why it got so far away from me."

Life often resembles a puzzle, with its intricate pieces scattered across the landscape of our experiences. Each piece represents a facet of our identity, our desires, and our journeys. In moments of reflection, we may find ourselves grappling with feelings of incompleteness, as if crucial pieces of our puzzle have been misplaced. However, rather than becoming anxious about filling those gaps, we can embrace a new perspective: the opportunity to explore the reasons behind our disconnections.

This journey of self-discovery encourages us to delve deeper into our past and understand the factors that have influenced our paths. Each missing piece symbolizes not a failure, but a lesson learned, a moment of growth, or a decision that shaped us. By cultivating curiosity about our experiences, we can transform our feelings of loss into opportunities for insight. This shift in mindset allows us to approach our lives with a sense of wonder, eager to uncover the lessons hidden within our struggles.

As we navigate through the missing pieces of our puzzles, we may find that the process of exploration is just as valuable as the final picture. The willingness to understand why we feel scattered opens doors to healing and self-acceptance. It encourages us to ask the right questions and seek the truth that lies beneath our anxieties. In this journey, we can develop a deeper connection with ourselves, learning to embrace our complexities and imperfections.

Ultimately, life's puzzle does not demand a perfect completion; rather, it invites us to appreciate the beauty of the process. Each piece, whether found or lost, contributes to the mosaic of our existence. By embracing the journey and remaining open to discovery, we can cultivate resilience and wisdom. In doing so, we find that the scattered pieces are not obstacles to be overcome, but essential parts of a larger narrative that we are continually writing.

Pause and Reflect

FOCUSING ON WHAT I CAN DO

"The list of things I cannot do is extensive.
So, I find it wise and helpful to only
focus on the things I can do.
Today I encourage you to do the same."

t is easy to become overwhelmed by the vastness of our limitations. The list of things we cannot do can feel like a heavy weight, dragging us down and clouding our vision. However, this acknowledgment of our limitations can serve as a catalyst for empowerment when we shift our focus. Instead of fixating on what lies beyond our grasp, we can redirect our energy towards the possibilities that exist within our reach. This is where true growth begins.

By concentrating on our strengths, we unlock the potential that resides within us. Each small accomplishment, every step taken towards our goals, serves as a reminder of our capabilities. This practice of focusing on the achievable allows us to cultivate a mindset of positivity and possibility. When we celebrate our victories, no matter how minor they may seem, we create a foundation for future success. This approach encourages resilience, enabling us to face challenges with confidence and determination.

Today, I invite you to join me in this transformative practice. As we move through our daily lives, let us consciously choose to highlight our strengths and capabilities. It may involve creating a list of things we can do, acknowledging our talents, and reminding ourselves of past accomplishments. This simple act can serve as a powerful motivator, urging us to act and embrace new opportunities.

In focusing on what we can do, we invite a sense of clarity and purpose into our lives. Rather than being hindered by feelings of inadequacy, we become active participants in our journeys. This perspective shift can lead to greater fulfillment and joy, as we learn to appreciate our unique contributions to the world. So, let us release the burdens of our limitations and embrace the empowerment that comes from focusing on our capabilities. Together, we can navigate our paths with courage and grace.

Pause and Reflect

Week Thirty Six

SEPTEMBER ROMANCE

"

"September seems like a great month to fall in love but break it up sometime around December as part of my New Year resolution."

118 | *Phara Lacombe*

September, marked by the arrival of autumn, symbolizes fresh starts and cozy connections—a perfect time to dive into romance as the world slows down and cools. Yet, the choice to "break it up around December" infuses an amusing twist, underscoring the transient, almost seasonal quality of some connections. It humorously suggests that, just like with New Year's resolutions, some relationships might serve us only temporarily.

Beneath the whimsy lies a deeper truth: not every romance is designed to last forever. Just as seasons change, so too do the connections we form.

The notion of a "relationship plan" nods to the importance of self-awareness and emotional clarity, allowing us to embrace love in all its warmth while also recognizing when it's time to let go. This playful perspective reminds us that it is perfectly natural to prioritize our happiness and growth—even if that means stepping away from a once-sweet romance. Ultimately, it invites us to savor the joy and intention in each connection, honoring what it brings to our lives, even if only for a season.

Pause and Reflect

THE COURAGE TO CHEER FOR OTHERS

"Some will not support you out of fear you might be successful. May God give them the strength to face and overcome their fear."

Fear can manifest in subtle ways, creating barriers that prevent others from embracing or celebrating someone else's success. At times, the fear isn't rooted in dislike or malice but stems from insecurities whispering, "What does their success mean for me?" This insecurity often creates a mindset where others feel threatened by someone embarking on a similar path, mistaking shared journeys for competition.

It's essential to remind ourselves—and others—that another person's progress does not diminish our own. There is enough space in the world for everyone to flourish, even in the same endeavors. In fact, having others join us on our journey can enhance the experience, offering collaboration, shared insights, and mutual encouragement.

Instead of harboring resentment or feeling overshadowed, we are called to choose grace. Pray for those who struggle with these fears, asking God to grant them the strength to overcome their insecurities. Let us hope they realize that lifting others doesn't take away from their own light—it only brightens the path for everyone.

When we shift our mindset from scarcity to abundance, we can embrace the beauty of shared success. It's okay for someone else to walk the same road or pursue the same dreams as us; their journey doesn't threaten ours. On the contrary, it may even serve as inspiration or a reminder that we're all capable of achieving greatness in our own way.

This reflection invites us to foster unity instead of division, to see others' victories as a collective triumph, and to recognize that together, we rise higher. By choosing understanding over fear and collaboration over competition, we open ourselves to a world where success is celebrated, shared, and multiplied.

Pause and Reflect

Week Thirty Eight

THE QUEST FOR REST

"

"I have a real relation-sleep problem;
I cannot seem to get enough."

The struggle with sleep is a common thread woven into the fabric of our modern lives. In a world that never seems to pause, the quest for restful slumber often feels elusive, like a fleeting dream just beyond our reach. This "relation-sleep problem" reflects more than just physical exhaustion; it reveals the deeper anxieties and demands that occupy our minds. The desire for connection, peace, and rejuvenation intertwines with our need for rest, creating a complex relationship with sleep that deserves our attention.

Acknowledging this challenge is the first step toward understanding its impact on our lives. Sleep deprivation not only affects our physical well-being but also infiltrates our emotional and mental health. The consequences can ripple through our relationships, our work, and our overall sense of self. By recognizing the importance of sleep and its role in our overall health, we empower ourselves to act. We can create routines that honor our need for rest, allowing us to recharge and reconnect with our true selves.

The quest for adequate sleep invites us to prioritize self-care in a world that often demands more than we can give. It is an opportunity to cultivate mindfulness, establishing boundaries that allow us to disconnect from the chaos of daily life. This intentionality can transform our relationship with sleep, turning it into a sanctuary rather than a source of stress. By nurturing our bodies and minds, we create a harmonious balance that fosters well-being and vitality.

Ultimately, addressing our "relation-sleep problem" is a journey of self-discovery and care. It serves as a reminder that rest is not a luxury but a necessity. As we navigate our daily lives, let us honor our need for sleep and recognize its profound impact on our overall health. May we strive to create environments that promote restful nights, allowing us to awaken each day refreshed and ready to embrace the opportunities that await us.

Pause and Reflect

_____

_____

_____

_____

_____

_____

_____

_____

_____

_____

_____

_____

_____

_____

_____

_____

_____

_____

_____

_____

_____

_____

_____

Week Thirty Nine

BLESSINGS IN THE DARKNESS

"My blessings came on good days. My blessings also came on long sleepless days, days filled with anxiety and unknown of what tomorrow will bring. Days of uncertainty and days filled with a weakness so deep in my bones, I can feel my heart and stomach caving in, days of mustering for the worst and praying to God. I do not see that day, because I do not have an alternate plan. Days that felt gloomy, days I cried alone but wore a smile for everyone else. Days I felt powerless and helpless; on that day, my blessings came. May your blessings always come when you need it the most."

Life's blessings often reveal themselves in the most unexpected moments. On the surface, we may find joy and gratitude during our brightest days, but it is the struggles that truly illuminate our path. The long, sleepless nights filled with anxiety, uncertainty, and deep-seated weakness can feel overwhelming, yet it is during these challenging times that we often find our greatest blessings. They remind us of our resilience, our capacity to endure, and the strength we possess to navigate life's trials.

During our darkest days, we may feel powerless, yet it is essential to recognize that this feeling is often a prelude to growth. It is in these moments of vulnerability that we learn to lean on our faith and the support of others. As we muster the courage to face our fears, we discover that blessings can emerge even when hope seems distant. They come in the form of small victories, unexpected kindness, or the comfort of knowing we are not alone. This shift in perspective allows us to embrace our struggles as integral parts of our journey.

Wearing a smile for the world while grappling with inner turmoil can be exhausting. Yet, it is often during these times of silent suffering that we cultivate the deepest connections with ourselves and others. Our vulnerability becomes a source of strength, allowing us to forge bonds based on authenticity and understanding

Pause and Reflect

BE THE EXAMPLE OF CHANGE

"

"Remember you are not God; you cannot change people. The only thing you can do is be the example of what change looks like, so that way if someone desires to change, they can look at you and know it's attainable."

We often find ourselves wishing for the power to change others. We want to see friends, family, and loved ones transform into the best versions of themselves, reflecting the growth we wish to inspire. However, we must confront a fundamental truth: we are not God, and we cannot change people. The power of transformation lies within everyone, and our role is not to force change but to embody it ourselves. By becoming living examples of what change looks like, we create a safe space where others can explore their potential for transformation. Our actions, behaviors, and mindset can serve as a beacon, illuminating the path for those who seek a similar journey.

Being an example of change requires authenticity. It calls for us to be genuine in our growth, to openly share our struggles and victories, and to exhibit the traits we wish to see in others. When we face challenges with grace, display resilience in the face of adversity, and consistently strive for improvement, we communicate a powerful message: change is not only possible but also attainable. This becomes especially meaningful in our relationships, where our growth can inspire those around us to embark on their journeys. By showing compassion and understanding, we foster an environment where change is welcomed and encouraged, allowing others to feel comfortable taking their first steps.

Moreover, the journey of change is deeply personal and unique to everyone. While we may wish to motivate others, we must also respect their timelines and processes. Each person's path may differ; some may take longer to recognize the need for change, while others may need time to develop the courage to act. In our role as examples, we must practice patience and support, understanding that our influence might be subtle but profound. By being present, offering encouragement, and maintaining our commitment to personal growth, we can serve as guiding lights in their journeys without imposing our will upon them.

Ultimately, the most significant impact we can have on others is through our own commitment to change. We must embrace the notion that our transformation may be the spark that ignites someone else's journey. By choosing to be the change we wish to see, we not only elevate ourselves but also uplift those around us. In doing so, we create a ripple effect, encouraging a culture of growth and transformation that can extend far beyond our immediate circles. Let us remember that while we cannot change others, we can certainly inspire them by living our truths, demonstrating that change is possible and, most importantly, attainable.

Pause and Reflect

Week Forty One

THE PATH TO WINNING

"

"You will make mistakes, you will stumble,
you will fail on your way to becoming a winner.
Stay the course."

Embracing the path to success is a journey filled with obstacles, setbacks, and moments of uncertainty. In the pursuit of our dreams, we are bound to make mistakes, stumble, and even fail. However, it is essential to understand that these experiences are not merely roadblocks but integral components of the journey toward becoming a winner. Each misstep provides valuable lessons that help us grow and refine our approach. The key lies in maintaining our resolve and staying the course, regardless of the challenges that may arise. A true winner understands that success is not a straight path; it is often a winding road filled with detours and unexpected turns.

Staying the course requires resilience—a steadfast commitment to our goals and a willingness to learn from our experiences. When we encounter failures, it can be tempting to throw in the towel, to question our abilities, or to doubt our dreams. However, it is precisely in these moments of doubt that our character is tested. We must remind ourselves that winners are not those who never fail; they are those who refuse to be defeated by their failures. By cultivating a growth mindset, we can transform setbacks into steppingstones, allowing us to adapt and evolve. This resilience not only strengthens our resolve but also deepens our understanding of ourselves and our aspirations.

Moreover, the journey to success often requires patience and perseverance. In a world that glorifies instant gratification, it is easy to lose sight of the long-term vision in favor of immediate results. However, true success is built on a foundation of hard work and dedication. Every small victory, every ounce of effort, accumulates over time, leading us closer to our ultimate goals. We must learn to celebrate these small wins, recognizing that they are milestones on our journey rather than distractions from our path. By maintaining a focus on our vision and consistently putting in the effort, we lay the groundwork for sustainable success.

In the end, the journey to becoming a winner is not defined solely by the accolades we receive or the goals we achieve. It is shaped by our resilience, our willingness to learn from our failures, and our unwavering commitment to our dreams. We must embrace the challenges, knowing they are integral to our growth. As we navigate this journey, let us remember that success is not a destination but a continuous process of self-discovery, growth, and perseverance.

Pause and Reflect

WHERE YOU TRAVERSE MATTERS

"

"Where ever you travel, bring your
inner light with you."

The path we choose to traverse in life significantly shapes our experiences and outcomes. Whether we are navigating our personal relationships, career choices, or individual goals, each step we take reflects our values, aspirations, and desires. It is essential to be mindful of our journey and the environments we immerse ourselves in. Every situation we find ourselves in holds potential lessons, and the company we keep can either elevate us or hinder our progress. The idea that "where you traverse matters" urges us to reflect on the significance of our surroundings and the people we allow into our lives.

As we navigate the various paths available to us, we must recognize that our choices can have far-reaching implications. For instance, surrounding ourselves with individuals who support our ambitions can foster an environment of growth, encouragement, and collaboration. Conversely, associating with those who undermine our efforts or encourage negativity can create a toxic atmosphere that stifles our potential. The essence of this reflection lies in recognizing the power of choice; by selecting our paths wisely, we set the stage for a fulfilling and purposeful journey. It is imperative to seek out spaces and relationships that nurture our growth rather than those that detract from it.

Additionally, traversing the right paths often requires courage and conviction. It can be tempting to settle for familiarity or comfort, even when we know it may not serve our best interests. True growth occurs outside of our comfort zones, and stepping into the unknown often leads to the most profound experiences. Embracing change and uncertainty can be daunting, yet it is within these moments that we discover our resilience and potential. By consciously choosing to venture into new territories, we open ourselves to opportunities for learning and self-discovery. This courage to explore uncharted paths not only broadens our horizons but also enriches our lives with meaningful experiences.

Ultimately, our journey is uniquely ours, shaped by the choices we make and the paths we choose to traverse. As we reflect on where we direct our energy and intentions, we empower ourselves to create lives filled with purpose and fulfillment. The journey may not always be easy, but it is within our power to navigate it with intention. Let us embrace the beauty of the journey, acknowledging that where we traverse matters, and may we choose paths that lead us toward growth, joy, and self-actualization.

Pause and Reflect

BE THE CHANGE
YOU WISH TO SEE

"

"Keep an open mind. Have an open heart,
but do not lose yourself and your purpose."

We live in a world that often calls for change—change in how we treat each other, in our communities, and in the wider systems around us. But to effect real transformation, we must first be the embodiment of that change ourselves. This quote is a powerful reminder that true influence begins within. It is easy to point fingers, to demand others adjust, or wish for the world to be different, but the real work starts by cultivating the qualities and values we seek.

When we commit to being the change, we are setting an example that others can see, feel, and connect with. This is a choice to lead not through loud demands or expectations of others but through consistent actions that reflect our ideals. It's about demonstrating kindness, integrity, and empathy in ways that ripple outward, inspiring others naturally, without force.

In embracing this approach, we give ourselves permission to grow, to falter, and to get back up again—all while keeping our vision of a better world close to heart. We realize that our lives are not just individual stories but threads in a vast tapestry that we help shape. By living out the change we wish to see, we elevate not only our own lives but contribute to the collective progress we hope for. Each of us is a spark, and when we choose to shine brightly, we light the way forward for others.

In being the change, we are reminded that we hold immense power to influence the world—not by expecting others to make it better, but by taking small, daily actions toward the world we envision. True transformation happens when enough of us make this choice, one step at a time, until the world we've dreamed of becomes the world we live in.

Pause and Reflect

BREAK UP IF YOU MUST, BUT NEVER CHEAT

66

"Life gets easier, you know.
The pain and the betrayal ease out of
your heart slowly you know.
The crisis eventually settles,
you know. Please give yourself time."

Ending a relationship is never easy, but the pain of breaking up pales in comparison to the betrayal of infidelity. Trust is the foundation of any healthy relationship, and once broken, it can be almost impossible to repair. While a breakup can be heartbreaking, it also offers a clean slate—a chance for both individuals to heal, grow, and seek new beginnings. Cheating, however, creates emotional wounds that linger, complicating not only the relationship but also the personal growth of both parties involved. It is better to walk away with integrity than to stay and deceive.

The temptation to cheat often arises from unspoken needs, unresolved frustrations, or a desire for excitement. Yet, giving in to this temptation erodes not just the trust within the relationship but also self-respect. A fleeting thrill is not worth the damage inflicted on a partnership built on love, respect, and commitment. True intimacy requires vulnerability and trust, and the moment one partner steps outside that sacred bond, it becomes difficult to regain what was lost. Relationships flourish when both individuals prioritize honesty and loyalty, even in moments of difficulty.

It is essential to recognize that challenges are a natural part of every relationship, but they must be met with communication and mutual effort, not betrayal. Passion can fade, and routines can feel stifling, but these moments offer an opportunity for growth rather than escape. Rekindling intimacy, being open about needs, and rediscovering shared passions can reignite the connection between partners. Relationships require continuous nurturing—an investment in each other's happiness and a shared commitment to evolve together, rather than seeking fulfillment outside.

In the end, walking away with dignity is far less destructive than staying in a relationship while compromising its core values. A breakup may bring sadness, but it also brings clarity and the freedom to rebuild. Cheating, on the other hand, leaves scars that take much longer to heal. It is better to face the discomfort of an honest goodbye than to carry the weight of dishonesty. In love, as in life, integrity must come first. If the bond no longer serves both partners, the bravest thing to do is part ways with respect and grace.

Pause and Reflect

WINNERS ARE THOSE WHO STAY THE COURSE

"Happy Wins-Day

On this WinsDay if you have "99 problems"

I pray "being" yourself ain't 1."

The journey to success is rarely smooth. It is filled with setbacks, missteps, and moments of self-doubt. But winners are not those who avoid failure—they are those who persevere through it. Staying the course means understanding that every failure carries within it the seeds of success. When we remain committed to our dreams, even when the path gets difficult, we cultivate resilience. This ability to persist, despite the challenges, is what distinguishes winners from those who give up too soon.

Failure is not a sign of defeat but a necessary part of the learning process. Every time we stumble, we gain insights that bring us closer to our goals. Winners understand that setbacks are opportunities for growth—they sharpen their focus, adjust their strategies, and keep moving forward. The road may be winding, and progress may feel slow, but every small step counts. Consistent effort, even in the face of adversity, builds the momentum necessary for long-term success.

Staying the course also requires a shift in mindset—from seeking immediate gratification to embracing the long game. True success is not achieved overnight; it is the result of continuous effort over time. Winners celebrate the small victories along the way, recognizing them as milestones in a much larger journey. This practice of gratitude keeps the spirit alive, motivating us to push forward even when the end goal seems distant. Persistence, paired with patience, creates an unstoppable force.

Ultimately, being a winner is less about the destination and more about who we become along the way. It is the journey— the growth, the lessons, the perseverance—that defines success. When we embrace every step, whether smooth or challenging, we gain a deeper understanding of ourselves and our purpose. Winners stay the course because they know that each moment, no matter how difficult, contributes to the person they are becoming. And in this commitment to growth, they inspire others to do the same.

Pause and Reflect

Week Forty Six

THE PATH YOU WALK DETERMINES YOUR DESTINATION

"

"The heart is the same, but it beats differently now.

The ears are the same, but it now hears
what is insinuated but not said.

The eyes are the same, but the vision is more defined.

The brain is the same, but the perceptions are changed.

You must embrace these changes, to be transformed."

The paths we choose to walk in life shape not only our experiences but also our destinations. Whether in relationships, careers, or personal growth, every decision we make reflects our priorities and values. Walking the right path requires discernment—being mindful of the environments we enter and the company we keep. The people and spaces we engage with either uplift us or pull us down. It is essential to surround ourselves with those who align with our purpose and nurture our growth.

The influence of our environment cannot be underestimated. Just as fertile soil nurtures healthy plants, supportive relationships foster personal development. Conversely, toxic surroundings can stunt our progress, leaving us feeling drained and unfulfilled. Walking with intention means being selective about who we allow into our lives and what paths we commit to. Every encounter and experience hold the potential to either propel us forward or hold us back, and the responsibility lies with us to choose wisely.

Sometimes, the right path is not the easiest. Growth often requires us to step into the unknown, leaving behind comfort and familiarity. It takes courage to venture into new territories, but this is where the most meaningful growth occurs. Challenges along the way are not signs of failure but opportunities to discover our strengths. By embracing uncertainty and trusting in the journey, we open ourselves to unexpected opportunities and deeper self-understanding.

Ultimately, life is a series of choices, and the path we walk determines where we end up. It is not enough to dream of success or happiness; we must actively pursue it by making decisions aligned with our values and goals. The beauty of this journey lies in its unpredictability—every twist and turn contributes to our story. When we walk with purpose and intention, we not only shape our own destiny but also inspire others to find their path. Let us choose our steps carefully, for the path we walk today becomes the foundation of our future.

Pause and Reflect

Week Forty Seven

THE SPLENDOR OF CHANGE

"

"Nothing is set in stone, that's the splendor of life; each day you have an opportunity to redefine your purpose, your goals, and your life."

Life is an evolving masterpiece, offering us the freedom to rewrite our story every day. Nothing binds us to yesterday's mistakes or outdated dreams, and that's the beauty of it. Whether we experience triumphs or setbacks, each morning is a new canvas waiting for us to paint with fresh aspirations. There is no shame in adjusting your goals or shifting your purpose; growth demands it. What may have served you in one season might no longer align with where your heart is pulling you now—and that's okay.

God's gift of free will is a reminder that we are not confined to the decisions we made in the past. The divine generosity of choice allows us to pivot when we need to and even start over if that feels right. Life is not a straight line but a series of twists, turns, and restarts. Sometimes the detours teach us more than the main road ever could. Our purpose is fluid, and with every experience, we gain more clarity about who we are and where we are meant to go.

Redefining your life isn't a sign of failure but of courage. It takes strength to let go of what no longer serves you and embrace new possibilities. Whether it's a career change, a shift in relationships, or a new personal mission, these adjustments allow us to grow into who we are meant to be. The gift lies in knowing that we always have permission to pivot when our spirit calls for change.

Each adjustment is an opportunity to align ourselves more closely with God's plan for our lives. Free will is abundant, not limited, and it is within this abundance that we discover true freedom. Our responsibility is to seek what brings us closer to peace and purpose—without fear of judgment or regret.

Pause and Reflect

MIND YOUR BUSINESS, MIND YOUR LIFE

"Mind your talent, mind your intelligence, mind your goals, and mind your time."

In a world full of distractions, it is essential to be mindful of what truly matters—your gifts, your ambitions, and the time you must pursue them. When you cultivate your talents with care, they grow into something extraordinary. Your intelligence, too, deserves attention, for it is a tool that sharpens with use. Being intentional about these things will leave little room for unnecessary distractions.

Time is perhaps the most precious resource we are given, and how we use it reflects the value we place on our lives. Those who guard their time wisely understand that it is the key to achieving their goals. When you mind your own path with focus and intention, you become too engaged in your growth to be concerned with other people's business. The energy once wasted on comparison or gossip can now be directed toward personal fulfillment.

Minding your goals requires consistency and clarity. It's not enough to dream; you must plan, act, and stay accountable to yourself. Every step, no matter how small, brings you closer to your destination. The discipline to stay the course creates a sense of fulfillment that external validation can never provide. Your goals are personal, and their success is measured only by how well they align with your values—not someone else's expectations.

Intelligence and talent are not fixed assets but gifts that flourish with practice and effort. To mind them well means to cultivate a mindset of lifelong learning. Each day offers a new opportunity to expand your knowledge and refine your skills. When you treat your abilities with care, they multiply, leaving you equipped to tackle challenges with confidence and grace.

In the end, living with intention ensures that your life reflects your purpose. Mind what matters most—your talent, intelligence, goals, and time. As you do, you'll discover that there is peace in staying on your own path, far from the distractions of other people's journeys.

Pause and Reflect

LOSING THE BATTLE, WINNING MYSELF

"I stopped fighting for love, understanding, commitment, and communication. I had put up a good fight, I was patient, I was hopeful. Somewhere along the way, I lost the battle but won myself."

There comes a time in life when you realize that not every battle is meant to be won. I fought for love with all the patience and hope I could muster, believing that if I held on long enough, things would change. I tried to bridge the gaps with understanding and open communication, but eventually, I reached a point where the effort became exhausting. Letting go was not easy, but it was necessary.

Losing the battle didn't mean I failed. In fact, it became a turning point—the moment I realized that the greatest victory is finding yourself. I discovered that love must begin within. I had spent so much time fighting for others that I lost sight of my own needs and worth. In choosing to let go, I made room for something far more valuable: self-love and peace.

God is just. He knows that sometimes we need to lose what we thought we wanted to gain what we truly need. Letting go is not about giving up; it's about releasing what is not meant for us to make room for what is. I found a deeper connection with myself, and in that connection, I rediscovered joy. It was as though God whispered, "It's time to come home to yourself."

Patience and hope are beautiful virtues, but they are not meant to keep us trapped in situations that deplete us. There is wisdom in knowing when to walk away. Not every door is meant to remain open, and not every relationship is meant to last forever. The loss was painful, but it was also liberating; I stopped waiting for others to show up for me and chose to show up for myself.

In winning myself, I found peace. I no longer need to fight for things that aren't freely given. God's justice lies in teaching us that we are enough as we are. The battles we lose sometimes lead us to the victories that matter most—the ones that happen within.

Pause and Reflect

GRATEFUL FOR THE JOURNEY

"

Today I woke up grateful, grateful for all the things I wanted that did not work out. It's God's plan, not mine. All I needed was to try, but it was always God's decision."

Gratitude has a remarkable way of reshaping our perspective on life's challenges. In our pursuit of dreams and desires, we often cling tightly to outcomes, believing that our worth is tied to success. However, waking up with a heart full of gratitude, especially for the things that did not come to fruition, is a profound realization. It reminds us that life unfolds according to a greater plan, one that may not always align with our expectations.

Embracing this truth requires us to surrender our need for control and trust in the divine timing of our lives. Each disappointment, every dream that remains unfulfilled, is a testament to the complexity of our journey. It is an invitation to reflect on the lessons we gleaned along the way. When we choose to be grateful for these experiences, we open ourselves to new possibilities, recognizing that what we perceive as setbacks may be redirections toward something greater.

In acknowledging that it is God's decision, we cultivate a sense of peace within ourselves. This acceptance allows us to release the burdens of regret and worry, freeing our minds to focus on the present. We learn to appreciate the efforts we made, understanding that trying is, in itself, a victory. This shift in mindset fosters resilience, empowering us to face future challenges with a renewed spirit, knowing that our worth is not defined by outcomes but by our willingness to engage wholeheartedly.

As we navigate our lives, let us carry this sense of gratitude with us. By embracing the lessons learned from our unmet desires, we become more attuned to the unfolding of our journeys. Trusting in a higher plan grants us the freedom to pursue our passions without fear, allowing us to celebrate the beauty of each moment, whether it meets our expectations or not. Today, may we find joy in the journey, knowing that we are exactly where we are meant to be.

Pause and Reflect

_____

_____

_____

_____

_____

_____

_____

_____

_____

_____

_____

_____

_____

_____

_____

_____

_____

_____

_____

_____

_____

_____

Week Fifty One

BLESSINGS BEYOND EXPECTATIONS

"Some closest to you will give their business far away. Some far away will give their business to you. Do not lose time nor productivity becoming disappointed; this too is God's way of providing. Contrary to how you expected this provision; be grateful for the provision you're receiving, for that is your blessing and your sustenance at this time. Maintain the attitude of 'my glass is always half full' with the understanding that God does it His way, not your way. May your business receive a boost this upcoming week."

Sometimes, the support we expect from those closest to us doesn't come. It's easy to feel hurt or betrayed when people we rely on choose to invest their energy elsewhere. However, this reflection reminds us that such experiences are not setbacks but part of a greater plan. God's provision often arrives from unexpected places, and rather than dwelling on the disappointment of unmet expectations, we are invited to be grateful for the blessings we receive—no matter their source.

The encouragement to avoid wasting time on frustration highlights the value of emotional discipline. Disappointments are inevitable, but our ability to stay productive and focused determines how quickly we recover and move forward. The world of business and life requires resilience—being able to pivot when things don't go according to plan. There is wisdom in accepting that God's timing and methods may differ from our expectations, but they are always purposeful. When we let go of how we think things *should* happen, we open ourselves to the abundance that is already present.

The mindset of seeing the glass as "always half full" is a call to gratitude, no matter the circumstances. A positive outlook does not mean denying hardships but choosing to recognize the good within them. When we adopt this attitude, we shift from scarcity thinking to abundance. This shift helps us remain calm, focused, and grateful, even when the outcome is different from what we anticipated. Trusting God's plan allows us to release the burden of controlling every detail and embrace what is unfolding, knowing it serves our growth and sustenance.

Ultimately, this reflection teaches us that every provision is valuable, regardless of how or where it comes from. It challenges us to let go of our limited perspectives and embrace divine timing. God's ways are higher than ours, and when we trust that what we have is exactly what we need in the moment, we experience a deeper sense of peace. The encouragement that "your business will receive a boost" serves as a reminder that blessings are always on their way; we simply need to remain open to receiving them in unexpected forms. Excitement of starting something fresh as summer fades and autumn ushers in cozy, romantic vibes. However, the abrupt suggestion to "break it up around December" introduces an amusing twist, implying that love—like other aspects of life—can be managed according to personal plans.

Pause and Reflect

GLOWING THROUGH THE DARKNESS

"God's people glow in the dark."

There is a light within God's people that no darkness can extinguish. Even in the face of persecution, betrayal, or lies, those who walk with God carry a radiance that shines through the shadows. The source of this glow is God Himself, for He is light. His love illuminates our paths, and His presence sustains us through the darkest moments.

When trials come, the glow within us grows brighter. Adversity is not a sign of abandonment but an opportunity for God to show His faithfulness. Just as stars shine most brilliantly against the night sky, our faith radiates most powerfully during difficult times. We may feel overwhelmed, but God's light within us provides strength and clarity, guiding us through every challenge.

God's people are not defined by circumstances but by the light they carry. This glow is not merely for personal comfort—it serves as a beacon for others. In a world full of darkness, our faith shines as a testimony to God's love and power. Even when others plot against us, God's light ensures that no weapon formed against us will prosper.

There is a quiet peace in knowing that no matter what comes our way, we are never without light. This glow is evidence of God's promise to be with us always. When we walk in alignment with Him, we become reflections of His goodness. His light within us is not temporary or conditional—it is eternal, shining through every season of life.

So, let us continue to walk boldly, knowing that God's light within us cannot be dimmed. We glow not because life is easy, but because God is good. In every trial, in every moment of joy, and in every season of waiting, His light sustains us. And as long as we carry His light, we will always find our way, no matter how dark the path becomes.

Pause and Reflect

SUMMARY

Allow *Vast Wisdom* to be your guide to inner strength and clarity. My hope is that this book will ignite a spark within you to capture and reflect on your own thoughts, dreams, and aspirations. There is remarkable power in the conversations we have with ourselves—the power to shape who we become and the impact we make in the world.

This collection is not just a series of quotes but an invitation to dive deeper into the essence of life itself. It's a blend of my insights, lessons, and experiences, gathered over years of observing, learning, and growing. Each quote is a piece of wisdom meant to inspire you toward new possibilities and renewed purpose.

In my journey, I have found inspiration in life's small details, in the people I meet, and in the raw beauty of human experience. Every day is not a good day, but each one brings a unique lesson, and that's what gives life its depth and meaning. I am honored to have you walk this path with me as I embrace the discovery phase of my own journey.

If you have ever wondered whether your talents and dreams are enough, or if your voice matters, let this book remind you that they do. Let *Vast Wisdom* be a companion on your path to greatness, encouraging you to rise, to speak truth into your life, and to take bold steps toward the vision that calls to you.

ABOUT THE AUTHOR

Phara Joassaint's journey reflects a remarkable blend of ambition, excellence, and creative expression, defining her as a powerful example of purposeful living. Born in Haiti, Phara has carried her cultural values of hard work, family devotion, and community service with her throughout her life. With an early career that started in banking as a teller at People's Bank, she quickly demonstrated her adaptability and skill, which saw her rise to Head Teller at Fleet Bank. But more than her professional accomplishments, Phara has shown a profound commitment to family, prioritizing her sons Leo and Alex's upbringing with intention and sacrifice. She carefully crafted her work schedule to ensure they had a parent present, even pausing her career to stay home during their formative years.

Her dedication to family went hand-in-hand with her expanding expertise in the financial world. As she progressed to roles with Citizens Bank and Regions, she never lost sight of her goal: to uplift others and provide stability for her family. Eventually, her career pivoted towards mortgage lending, where her 13 years as a Licensed Mortgage Loan Originator highlighted her passion for helping families build their futures. This path led her to launch Vast Mortgage, a mortgage brokerage firm grounded in her belief in empowerment and transparency. As a mortgage broker and business owner, Phara combines her financial expertise with genuine care, guiding clients through one of life's most significant investments.

In addition to her business achievements, Phara is a gifted singer and songwriter, infusing her music with heartfelt messages that resonate with themes of resilience, faith, and connection. Her songs have become a form of storytelling, allowing her to reach others on a deeply personal level. Through her music, she brings the same intensity and compassion to her audience that she brings to her business and family. Each song is crafted not only with lyrical and melodic skill but with the authenticity that characterizes all her endeavors.

Phara Lacombe's story is a demonstration of how one can harmonize professional success with personal values. Her journey encourages others to pursue their ambitions without compromising on what matters most. Phara is a living example of how true success is defined not only by career accomplishments but by the legacy of integrity, love, and purpose one leaves behind.

www.ingramcontent.com/pod-product-compliance
Lightning Source LLC
LaVergne TN
LVHW051235080426
835513LV00016B/1599